# All About Money

## By Erin Roberson

**Consultant**
Linda Bullock
Math Curriculum Specialist

Children's Press®
A Division of Scholastic Inc.
New York   Toronto   London   Auckland   Sydney
Mexico City   New Delhi   Hong Kong
Danbury, Connecticut

Designer: Herman Adler Design
Photo Researcher: Caroline Anderson
The photo on the cover shows children holding coins and a dollar.

**Library of Congress Cataloging-in-Publication Data**

Roberson, Erin.
  All about money / by Erin Roberson.
      p. cm. — (Rookie read-about math)
  Includes bibliographical references and index.
  ISBN 0-516-24420-5 (lib. bdg.)          0-516-24672-0 (pbk.)
  1. Money—Juvenile literature. I. Title. II. Series.
  HG221.5.R63 2004
  332.4—dc22
                                    2004005072

# Treasure sits at the bottom of the sea.

A diver looking for treasure

4

Long ago, long wooden ships sailed the sea. Some of these ships sank. Many carried coins and jewelry.

Coins are pieces of money.
People have used coins for
a long time. They still use
them today.

Some coins show pictures
of people or places. Others
show plants or animals.

This nickel has an animal on the back of it. 7

# People work at different jobs to earn money.

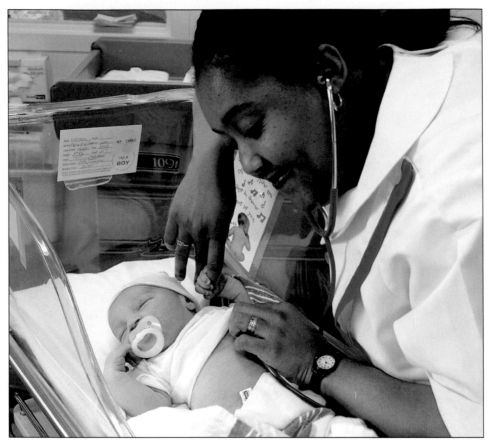

A nurse at work

A family at a bank

People save the money
they earn. They save
money in jars, cans,
banks, or piggy banks.

People spend money to
buy things, too.

There are pennies, nickels, dimes, quarters, and dollars.

A penny is one cent. It shows Abraham Lincoln.

He was the sixteenth president of the United States.

In the 1900s, someone could buy a tiny doll for only one penny.

What can you buy with a penny today?

Some gumballs cost a penny.

16

You can trade five pennies for one nickel.

A nickel is five cents. It is bigger than a penny. It shows Thomas Jefferson.

He was the third president of the United States.

In the 1900s, a person could buy a box of crayons for one nickel.

What can you buy with a nickel today?

These pencils cost a nickel.

19

You can trade two nickels for one dime.

A dime is ten cents. It is the smallest coin. It shows Franklin D. Roosevelt.

He was a president of the United States, too.

In the 1930s, a person could buy a comic book or a toy truck with one dime.

What can you buy for a dime today?

This toy dinosaur costs a dime.

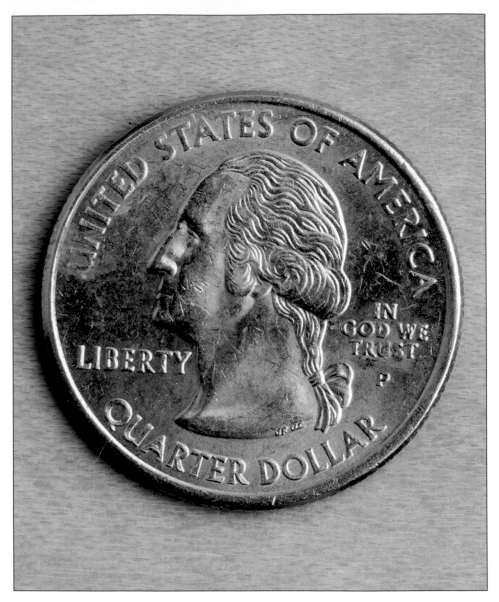

24

Two dimes and one nickel equal one quarter. A quarter is 25 cents.

A quarter is bigger than a penny, nickel, and dime. It shows George Washington.

He was the first president of the United States.

In the 1900s, a person could buy a family of teddy bears or a child's tea set for one quarter.

What can you buy for a quarter today?

You can trade 100 pennies, 20 nickels, 10 dimes, or 4 quarters for one dollar.

A dollar can be a coin, or a bill made of special paper.

What can you buy for one dollar today?

# Words You Know

dime

dollars

nickel

penny

quarter

# Index

# About the Author

Erin Roberson is a teacher and writer. She took her first job at the age of 16. She worked in a restaurant. There she learned to work a cash register and make change. Erin has been saving and spending coins ever since.

# Photo Credits